Clouds Running In

Kim Shuck

Drawings by

Marcer Campbell

PUBLISHED BY TAUREAN HORN PRESS
P. O. BOX 526
PETALUMA, CA 94953
ISBN 978-0-931552-16-8

Acknowledgements

THE FOLLOWING POEMS HAVE
BEEN PREVIOUSLY PUBLISHED
IN THE FOLLOWING PUBLICATIONS:

CULTURALLY SENSITIVE EDUCATION, A BLANKET AS MAP
IN "DRUMVOICES REVIEW" ED. ODESSA BETHEA,
SPRING-SUMMER-FALL 2006 V. 14, NS. 1 AND 2

NOT STANDING AT THE BAR IN
"PARTHENON WEST REVIEW" ED. CHAD SWEENEY
AND DAVID HOLLER, V. 3, WINTER 2005

AWAY-THE WORK OF POETS IN WORDS UPON THE WATERS,
ED. KARLA BRUNDAGE, SARA BIEL AND KIM SHUCK,
JUKEBOX PRESS, JUNE 2006

CLOUDS ROLLING IN IN "LISTEN AND BE HEARD"
ED. MARTHA MIMS, JUNE 26, 2006

I ALWAYS CATCH THE OLD WORLD DISEASES IN
"LISTEN AND BE HEARD" ED. MARTHA MIMS, JULY 7, 2006

TALECRUMBS I LEFT MYSELF FOR NAVIGATION
IN "CURRENT ACCOUNTS" ISSUE 29, 2010

TABLE OF CONTENTS

For Grandma Mae, Bee and all of my kids collected, birthed or otherwise. Also for my South Eastern sisters wherever you've drifted. May you have all of what you need and a healthy amount of what you want.

Clouds

Running In

BECAUSE WHEN I SPEAK CHEROKEE IN PUBLIC IT MAKES SOME FOLKS NERVOUS

TODAY'S HISTORY LESSON WILL BE WRITTEN
BY ANTS
UNDER THE BARK OF A TREE
IN TILDEN PARK.
I WON'T KNOW HOW TO READ IT EITHER.

THIS FOG IS NOT
AN UNFAMILIAR FOG.
THE AFTERNOON'S WIND
HOT IN THE VALLEYS
WILL NOT BE UNFAMILIAR.
IN AUGUST THE
DIE OFF OF PAINTED LADIES
BUTTERFLIES PILED LIKE LEAVES
NOT UNFAMILIAR.
MORE BLACK THAN COPPER
ONE BLEACHES IN THE CAFE WINDOW
TONGUE CURLED
EYE SECTIONED INTO TINY MATTE BLACK TILES
GESTURED LIMBS
ARRESTED.

THAT GUY ACTUALLY LOOKED AT ME AS IF
I WOULD KNOW WHAT IT MEANT.
I LIVE HERE
NOW
LISTEN FOR THE OPENING OF PARKING PLACES,
MEASURE SPACE IN TINY MATTE GREY TILES.
THESE CALENDARS AREN'T COMPLETE
CEREMONIAL DATES COME
GRADUALLY INTO FOCUS.
SOME THINGS HERE ARE SO NEW THAT
NOTHING HAS FIGURED OUT HOW TO EAT THEM YET.

SMOKE AND BEAN SOUP

THE TRUST OF NEW THINGS OF
BAROQUE AND MECHANICAL SEED PODS EVEN
NOW WITH THESE DAYS ORANGING THE
FUMBLE OF UNCOMMITTED RAIN AND HANDMADE
BROOMS AND THE HUNT FOR HOLDOUT
CRUMBS THE
SUN COMING OUT IN THE AFTERNOON IN
SEDUCTIVE ANGLES AND AT
LEAST ONE HILLSIDE HERE STILL RISING WITH THAT
ANISE SMELL THESE VARIED NEW YEARS THESE
ESSENTIAL CEREMONIES GIFT BLANKETS
TUGGED CLOSE AMULETIC
FORTIFICATIONS OF SOUP-WARMED
SPOONS AND CHEEKS ON FLANNEL SHIRTS OF
APPLESAUCE THIS SEASON
RANSOMED WITH SPICES THIS
COPAL SMOKE THAT CARRIES MY
VERY REAL BELIEF THAT CAN
CURL EXACTLY AROUND CAN
BEAR THESE WORDS CAN
HISS SOFTLY THE SONGS OF
TRANSFORMING

NOT STANDING AT THE BAR

IMAGINE THAT ALL THE RUMORS YOU HAVE HEARD ARE TRUE.

ALL WEEK I KEEP MIXING UP MY WORD PROCESSOR AND MY
FOOD PROCESSOR.
THE COOKIES ARE SARCASTIC AND
I CAN'T GET ALL THE PAPER FROM BETWEEN MY TEETH.
OFF BALANCE
THAT'S ALL.

THE HILLS ARE WRINGING WET AND
GHOST RATS HAUNT THE FRINGE OF SHRUBS NEAR
THAT GAS STATION IN MARIN CITY.
EVERYWHERE THERE IS THE SOUND OF
WATER FINDING ITS LEVEL.
WE MUST BE SUBJECT TO IT TOO
FIND OURSELVES WALKING BELOW THE CREEK BED
TO THE BEACH.
I DON'T KNOW THIS CREEK.
SOMETHING HIT THE BRIDGE HARD THERE
PROBABLY IN THE LAST STORM
SHATTERED A BEAM
WHATEVER IT WAS
GONE NOW.

WE SIT ON A BENCH AND EAT SATSUMAS DOWNTOWN POINT
REYES STATION
IN THE CASUAL AND PROTECTIVE SLOUCH OF AN OLD BARN.
GETTING RAINED ON INDOORS.
THE WATER WILL SEEK YOU OUT.

HOW MANY TIMES HAVE WE BEEN OVER THIS BRIDGE?
HOW MANY BRIDGES DURING THIS TRIP?
I MISTRUST BRIDGES
SHORTCUTS OF ALL KINDS ARE SUSPECT.
AFTER ALL THERE ARE THE GHOST RATS
A WOMAN WITH A FINGERBONE SKIRT
ALWAYS SOME GUARDIAN AT THE TRANSITION.
WATER MUTTERING ABOUT THE BUSINESS OF
FINDING OTHER WATER.

THE DAY I GRADUATED TO STANDING AT THE BAR

WAS HANDED MY FIRST ADULT DRINK
IT WAS A BEER AND A WHISKEY.
THOSE SMALL DOSES
WE ARE TAUGHT TO TAKE.
TAUGHT ACCEPTABLE METHODS OF SELF-MEDICATION
USUALLY AT THE ELBOW OF A LOVED ONE.
SO I STOOD
UNTIL I COULDN'T STAND ANYMORE.
I'VE ALWAYS BEEN THE PROBLEM CHILD.
IT'S NOT BEING NAIVE
OR EVEN LAZY,
NOT MOST OF THE TIME.
IF YOU CAN HEAR THE WATER MUTTERING
CAN FIGURE OUT AN OFFERING TO THE GUARDIAN
CIGARETTE
ROCK
SEED OF SOME SORT
IF YOU FIND A WAY TO PASS SAFE
FIND THE FRUIT
FIND THE BAY THAT'S ALMOST ON THE ROAD
FIND BREAKFAST
IF YOU CAN FIND ME.
FIND ME.
I'LL GET IT WORKED OUT.
JUST REMEMBER ABOUT THE RUMORS
EVERY SINGLE ONE OF THEM IS TRUE.

CULTURAL EXCHANGE

BRING YOUR EXPECTATIONS
I'LL BRING BLOOD
SHOVEL INCISORS
MY PERSPECTIVE.
I'M SURE WE'LL FIND SOMETHING TO DO.

OUTLAW MY LANGUAGE THEN ASK ME TO SPEAK IT
A PARLOR TRICK
CLOSE UP MAGICIANS AND
TRANCE MEDIUMS
A BETTER SHOW.

PLAYING DARTS NEAR KING'S CROSS I ALMOST FOUND
SOMETHING
SOMETHING IN THE SONG OF YOUR SPEAKING
KEEP TALKING
I'VE NEARLY FIGURED IT OUT
TELL ME ANYTHING
TELL ME A BEDTIME STORY.
I DON'T THINK I'VE EVER MET ANYONE THAT BRAVE
BEFORE.
YOU LOOK YOURSELF RIGHT IN THE FACE DON'T YOU?

WRITING BREATH

1.
I DREAM OF WORDS
COMING UP
A COAGULATING MIST
FROM UNDER THE GROUND.
NEITHER A PRODUCT
OF HUMAN DESIRE TO BE UNDERSTOOD
NOR A DIVINE GIFT
BUT AN EXHALATION OF ROCK
WATER
AND WIND.
IN THIS DREAM I LEARN
TO WEAVE SNARES.

2.
WRITING MIGHT BE
THE TRACKS OF THINGS
WE SAY.
COULD BE
AN IMAGE OF SOUND
BEYOND
THE ONE WE SING
BREATHE OUT
INTO MITOCHONDRIAL
DNA.

LONG MAN WRITES HIS OWN
SOUND
INTO STREAM EDGES
HERE
AND IN UTAH
AN ART OF TIME, CERTAINLY.

3.
HARD TO MAKE AN
EXHALATION
INTO MARKS ON
PAPER

ROCK
PLASTIC
OR SKIN.
IT TAKES SOME
TOOL
THAT WILL
VIOLATE.

BACK TO CHEROKEE

A CREAMY LICK OF DOGWOOD
REDBUD
WILD WISTERIA
UNMANNERLY
PULLING SOME OTHER TREE DOWN.
RIVER WATER SEEMS HIGH ON THE TRUNKS.

MY LANGUAGE COMES FROM THIS PLACE
NEVER SEEN IT BEFORE
REFUGEE KIT OVER ONE ARM
I TAKE IT ALL IN.
LATER HOT RAIN
MUMBLES GREETING.

TWO CREPE MYRTLES
LOCUST TREES
ANOLES
BY THE POOL
ONE, THE MALE
STALKS US FROM A LOW WALL.

I COULD SIT QUIETLY BY A POND
WAIT FOR MYTHICAL CREATURES
I KNOW THEIR NAMES
THE RED HAWK
GIANT SNAKE
HERE NOW, I COULD BELIEVE IN ANYTHING.

A CANADIAN GOOSE
MOCKINGBIRDS
IN ELLEN'S CAR A SCARLET FLASH
TOO FAST BUT
PROBABLY A CARDINAL
EVER PRESENT ENGLISH SPARROWS.

HOME AND TOO SOON TO KNOW
THERE IS LAUNDRY
THERE ARE BILLS
IN MY HAND A MEDICINE BUNDLE
GIFT FROM THE STUDENTS
I SAY A PRAYER AND LET IT SLIP INTO THE FIRE.

A GARBAGE TRUCK WOKE ME

IT'S HARD TO KNOW WHAT WILL CHANGE THE WORLD
THE CHIME OF FAR OFF BIRDS
OR THE TAXI BACK-UP ALARM
AT 5:10 SOME
JULY MORNING

SINGING AT DAWN AGAIN
I TRY TO KNOW THIS PLACE BETTER
CORRIDOR OF FOG UP PARNASSUS
OVER ROCKY POINT
SLIPPING DOWN THE LOWER HAIGHT
INTO HAYES VALLEY
LIKE EVERYONE ELSE THROUGH CIVIC CENTER
TENDERLOIN NEAR MARY'S PLACE
PAST THE TURNAROUND
IT HEADS FOR THE BAY I THINK

MAY PULL AT IMAGINATION
BUT THERE ARE LOTS OF BIRDS
POSSUMS
COMIC RACCOONS
A TUMBLING ACT ON THE ROOF'S DARK

HAVE THE VERSION YOU WANTED
A MOUTHFUL OF CRAB
CAUGHT ELSEWHERE
MOCK PRISON SHIRTS
A DARING TURN TO WITNESS THE GUYS
EITHER WITH A GIGGLE OR A REAL INTEREST
OR MAYBE BOTH
SHOCKING IN ITS NORMALCY
FOLKS AT WORK OR
DRINKING COFFEE

I SCALE THE ARCHED INSTEP OF
A HILL
TAKE A STEM OF PRIMROSE SOUR GRASS
WE USED TO GATHER JAM BERRIES
BEFORE THE HOUSE WAS HERE

SOME EVIDENCE OF THE HUMAN

DAZED FROM THE COLLISION
A COLLECTION OF LADYBUGS
THEIR INEBRIATE FLIGHT
ENDING ON MY SWEATER
SPECKLED NOW
RED AND BLACK ON BLACK
I INTERRUPT RAVENS
SWEEPING IN THEIR
FULL-BODIED STRIDES
DOWN 18TH

AREN'T THERE ANY HUMAN PEOPLE?
IT'S FRIDAY

ABANDONED MARBLE SCRAP
A MANY YEARS PROJECT
TUMBLE WITH A SHOP VAC
ONLY ONE BIT INCOMPLETE
BEHIND THE BOUGAINVILLEA
CURRENTLY ENGAGED IN
FUCHSIA HYSTERICS
THE OTHER PLANT
SOME CLIMBER
WHITE BLOOMS
NOT PASSIONFLOWER I THINK

I'M PASSED BY AN ESCALADE
LACKS THE HUMAN
I HAD IN MIND
BUT EVIDENCE OF HUMAN
TINTED GLASS MAKE IT
MORE BEETLE THAN THE
LADYBUG THUGS FROM
MY EARLIER CRASH

INTO THE CAFÉ
NEARLY TWENTY ACTUAL HOMO SAPIENS
IN TRANSIT ON THE
INFORMATION SUPER HIGHWAY
ORDERS FOR COFFEE THE ONLY
UNMEDIATED INTERACTIONS

I PULL OUT MY PEN AND PAPER
AND OUT THE WINDOW
FLAME COLORED BIRDS
GOSSIP IN THE PUZZLE BARK TREE

HIDDEN ROOTS

PAVEMENT KNOWS A FEW THINGS ABOUT STREETS AND
SHOP WINDOW REFLECTIONS RESISTS THE PRESS AND SWELL OF
HIDDEN ROOTS RESISTS THE
CRACK AND CRACK OF PRYING RAIN THE CARESS OF SHOE AND
WHEEL HOLDS TO THE
WINDROSE OF ROADMAPS
HOLDS CLOSE

SONG WITH RELICS

I KNOW THAT THE LION ISN'T
SMILING AND THAT THIS SMOKE
CARRIES NO PRAYERS TO
SOME OVERSEER WHO MIGHT BE
KNOWN BY HORSE AND SWORD BUT NOT BY
DESERT OR PEN I HAVE READ YOU
SLEPT PILLOWED ON YOUR
WORDS AND
LONGED FOR PROPHESY IN WILDER
AIR NOW
STREAKED WITH THIS MEANINGLESS
SMOKE THIS WASTED
BURNING AND SOME OF US
TANGLE OUR FINGERS IN THE
SMOULDER AND DARKNESS SOME OF US
INTRODUCE OURSELVES

SO MUCH MORNING

SUCH ANGLED RAVENS IN THIS
CONGESTED SKY SUCH A WHITE
BLOUSE LEFT OVERNIGHT IN THE FOG THAT
MILKGLASS IMPULSE ABSORBED INTO
EMBROIDERY THREADS ONE AT A
TIME AND THE MEMORY
RAVEN MUTTERS APPROVINGLY

SUCH BREATH HERE BESIDE THE
TIPPED ROSEBUSH SUCH RED-ORANGE
BRICK IN HEAPS AND THE
DREAM RAVEN STEALS A SHINY
NOTION OF REUSE FOR A
LETTER HE IS WRITING IN SMALL
THIN GESTURES

SO THIN THE BORDERS MORNING
BUS SOUNDS OR NO THE JUST WAKED
RETINAL IMAGE OF A VERY LARGE AND NEARBY
WATERFALL SO STURDY LATE AND
ULTIMATELY USELESS UME SO
MARBLE THE BRIGHT
CRAB APPLES

SUCH A STILL AIR ON THIS
CRUST OF HARVEST TIME SO
CLAY THE SOIL IN THE OLD
CREEK BED SO WILD AN
OFFERING TOBACCO SUCH
SHARP RED BEADS SUCH A
HEARTFUL OF MINT SCENT

I HEAR US SINGING

THIS MORNING'S SONG FOR THOSE BORN
TO OTHER PEOPLE'S DREAMS
SO UNLIKELY
A FUNNY, LINGERING FOG
LIKE SPIES
WE KNOW EACH OTHER
IN THE LINES FOR THE BANK MACHINES
WHILE BUYING BOOKS OR COFFEE
OUR EYES CLASP AND SLIDE
NO ONE ELSE THE WISER

WE SING THESE MORNING SONGS
AT THE SITES OF PIPED CREEKS
SOMETIMES EVEN AT THE DRINKING FOUNTAIN
TOUCH OUR FACES WITH WATER
AND SING
I SAW YOU SINGING NEAR THE ART MUSEUM
STONE BLUSHING RED FROM NEW LIGHT
WE FELL INTO BRIEF DUET
ANONYMOUS, LOVING
CLANDESTINE

HARD TO KNOW IF WE WERE
WHAT THEY'D HAD IN MIND
PLANNING ALL THE WHILE
FOR US, NOT FOR THEMSELVES
SUCH A RESPONSIBILITY
THINGS WASH UP ON THE SHORE
DIG THEMSELVES INTO THE EDGES OF RIVER OUTLETS
WE CAN FIND THEM THERE
I CAN HEAR YOU SINGING
SOME MORNINGS

HOW TO BE ONE OF THE PEOPLE

DAD SENDS ME A POLITICAL JOKE
THROUGH E-MAIL
HE IS NORTH EASTERN OKIE TERSE
CAN SEE THE FAMILIAR MOUTH QUIRK
THE DUCK BEHIND A FOREHEAD CURL
I RETURN TO THE 70S

HIDE NIGHTGOWNS
HOPING
I'LL GET DADDY'S T-SHIRT INSTEAD
SOFT, WHITE
SMELLING OF OLD SPICE
PIPE SMOKE OR CIGARETTES
BEER OR CANE ALCOHOL

DAD SHIPPED OUT TO NAM
MID DR. NO
ON AN AIRCRAFT CARRIER
A VOLUNTEER
GESTURED BRAVERY
GENETIC POSSIBLY

GRAMPS DID IT TOO
CHASED ROMMEL AROUND NORTH AFRICA
HE COULD DO TRIG IN HIS HEAD
WAS STATIONED IN GERMANY
WHILE DAD WAS IN HIGH SCHOOL
LOVED MY GRAN WITH A LIGHT
THAT EMBARRASSED MY TEEN YEARS GRAMPS
DIED OF LEAD AND CADMIUM IN THE WATER

DAD QUIT SMOKING FOR MY KIDS
STILL TALKS LIKE A SMOKER
PAUSES
LICKS AN UPPER LIP
VOICE RUMBLING
READS LIKE AN OXFORD DON
STILL FEELS UNCOMFORTABLE
IN UNIVERSITIES
I DID MY DEGREE FOR DAD

ON ONE TRIP TO A LIQUOR STORE
I MUST HAVE BEEN AROUND 3
COUNTER GUY SAW MY BLOND CURLS
MY BROWN DAD'S BLACK ONES
ASKED ME IF HE WAS REALLY MINE
LATER DAD TAUGHT ME TO SEE
THE FUNNY IN THE SAD
GENTLY GRACEFUL
A FEATURE I SEE IN MY CUBS
IF NOT IN MYSELF

DAD SHOWED ME HOW TO BE ONE OF THE PEOPLE
ONE NIGHT HEADING FROM TULSA TO
PICHER
IN A RENTAL CAR
DARK
NEITHER OF US TALKING
KING OF THE ROAD
ON THE RADIO
HEAT THICK AIR
SOUND OF TIRES MEASURING GRAVEL

SACRED SPACES

YOU ARE ONE OF THE THINGS I DIDN'T
KNOW ABOUT CLOUDS ON THIS
BAS RELIEF MORNING
PRE-DAWN WITH THAT
MARKET CROSS MOON RIGHT THERE AND THE
TOUR OF PAST YOUR OLD HOUSE ISN'T
HELPING TODAY THIS SLEEP IS
STIRRED AND THE BANK CALLED TO
'SAVE ME MONEY' SO I'M
COUNTING MY FINGERS STILL THERE ARE
SOME THINGS THAT YOU CAN LOSE AND
REGAIN AND I'LL STAND ON ANY STAGE YOU
WANT AND SAY THAT WONDER IS ONE OF THEM
WONDER AND COMMUNITY AND THE
INVISIBLE MARK OF MY PALM ON THE
BOTTOM STEP OF THAT HOUSE AT THE ROOT OF COLLINGWOOD

SETTLEMENT

THEY IMAGINE
CURSED LAND
UNHOLY WITHOUT THEM
PURGE THE INDIGENOUS
MOVE ALL THE BIOTA
SORT THEM WITH SCIENCE
SHIP TO GARDENS
RELOCATION CAMPS
A ZOO
APPROPRIATE TO THEIR CLASSIFICATIONS
VIVISECT THE SYSTEM
GARDEN US
FENCE US
I'M STILL SLEEPING THIS DREAM
SOMEONE IN THE FAMILY
HAS BLOOD THAT CURES CANCER
WE'RE SENT AWAY FROM EACH OTHER
ALL OVER THE WORLD
SO THAT SOMEONE ELSE CAN GROW
CELERY IN THE DESERT

DHLA:NUWA

QUARTER TO SIX
WANTED TO WRITE TO YOU
ABOUT A RED BIRD
REALIZED
YOU DON'T KNOW MY STORIES
KNEW WE WERE YEARS FROM SHARING
THE ONE I NEEDED YOU TO HEAR

WE'RE MISPLACED
BOTH OF US
KEYS IN THE LEFT POCKET OF
A BORROWED JACKET
MISPLACED
BUT WITH TIME WE CAN
FIND OUR WAY AROUND TO IT

SLOW WORK
WE DO THIS
WORD BY WORD
EACH WORD A STORY
EVERY STORY BEADED
WITH WORDS
NO HURRY, IT'S ONLY QUARTER TO SIX.

SINGING AT MY LAPTOP

HALF AN HOUR AND MY TONGUE IS SORE
THE SOMETIMES UNFAMILIAR GEOMETRY OF THIS LANGUAGE
TURNS SOFT PARTS OF MY MOUTH TEMPORARILY TO STONE
I'M PICKING SAND FROM MY BACK TEETH HOURS LATER
THE OUTLAWS WHO DEFIED SCHOOL RULES
STOOD QUIET OR CRYING OR SCREAMING THROUGH THE
BEATING
MUST TASTE SMILES AT THIS SIGHT
SO MANY THINGS I CAN'T SAY
CAN'T THINK ABOUT
AROUND THESE BUSY BUSY VERBS
SIP MEDICINE FROM A LIGHTNING KILLED TREE
SLIPS GROW GREEN AROUND THE STUMP
SHRUG SHOULDERS
LOOSEN NECK
START SINGING AGAIN

UNCONTROLLED BURN

THE WEST IS BURNING
THEY DIDN'T KNOW
BUT MORE THAN THAT
DIDN'T LISTEN
AND FIRE WILL FIND
IT'S OWN LEVEL
SUSPENDED BETWEEN
ELIZABETHAN NOTIONS
EDENIC NAKEDNESS
VIRGINITY UNTOUCHED
UNNOTICED
AND THE MYTH OF
SAVAGERY
FOIL TO SUPERIOR
RECORD KEEPING
IMPOSSIBLE TO HEAR US
THEN
THE WEST IS BURNING
ON THE SIDEWALK
I'M ACCOSTED BY KIDS
"DO SOMETHING FOR THE ENVIRONMENT"
IT'S BURNING, I THINK
NO TIME TO TALK TO THEM
EXPLAIN
IT'S ENERGY FLOWING HOME
YOU WANT YOUR PAIN
PRODUCTIVE
DON'T UNDERSTAND THE
RELEASE
OF FIRE
WANT TO CHILDPROOF THE PLANET
IT IS DANGEROUS
YOU ARE IN DANGER
THERE IS BURNING
ALL THAT STUFF YOU KEPT
POTENTIAL ENERGY
AND DIFFICULT TO ORGANIZE

FIRE IS NO MOUSE
QUIETLY NIBBLING IN DARKNESS
THE WEST IS LIT
BUILD IN THE ACHING DRY
STORE KINDLING
AND HOPE AGAINST A SPARK

A BLANKET AS MAP

ART IS TERRITORIAL
THESE ASSEMBLIES OF THINGS
COLLECTED FROM MY WORLD
LIFTED FROM YOURS AND REWORKED
UNTIL THEY HAVE A PLACE IN MINE
NO LESS A STATEMENT THAN THE CAT
FACE RUBBING SCENT MARK
MIGHT FEEL GOOD
MIGHT FLATTER
PURR MIGHT PLEASE
DON'T BE FOOLED
THIS IS ABOUT TURF
THESE BLOODY PAWPRINTS
I STITCH ACROSS OUR SHARED QUILT

SONG

DRAPED IN THE
CUTWORK LACE OF
OVERHEAD WIRES AND
HICCUP SKYLINE THE WILD
CODE OF PHONE CALLS OF
CAR TIRES ON PAVEMENT THE
BORAGE SINGS BLUE TOMATO
PLANTS
BEAN PLANTS
MAYBE PEPPERS SPEAK LANGUAGES I
ALMOST UNDERSTAND BREATHE
BIRDS BREATHE
LANGUAGE BIRDS

TO A DIFFERENT WATERSHED

I MAKE SURE TO PACK A
MAP TURTLE SHELL
MAKE SURE
I BRING MY HANDS
TOOLS MAYBE
PEN
SHARPENED STICK

PACK POEMS
VOICE
TINY BITS OF GLASS
SORTED INTO SMALL
GOURDS
SOMETHING SOFT TO
CARVE WORDS INTO

I MAKE SURE TO PACK
WITH CARE
PROCESSING EQUIPMENT
THINGS I USE TO
KNOW THE SHADOWS
OF ANGLES
THE GEOMETRY OF YOUR PLACE

AWAY
THE WORK OF POETS

THERE WILL BE SONGS ABOUT THIS
ONCE BODIES ARE FOUND
COLLECTED
ONCE THEY ARE BURIED
ONCE GRAVE DIRT IS RINSED FROM HANDS OR
COLLECTED CAREFULLY
SET ASIDE FOR
RETRIBUTIVE INCANTATIONS
THEN THERE WILL BE SONGS

THINGS RETURN FROM AWAY
PLACE WE PUT THE UNWANTED
BACTERIA EMERGE
TRASH FLOATS FREE
SOME KIND OF UNSPECIFIED
POLLUTANT
CLOUDS THROUGH FLOODWATER
WE'LL PUMP IT ELSEWHERE
THE PEOPLE WILL BE MOVED

THERE WILL BE BANDS
FINERY
THERE WILL BE THE SOFTNESS OF SHELL
THERE WILL BE BRASS
WE WILL BRING OUT THE FEATHERS
THE BEADS
ONCE THE BABIES HAVE ENOUGH TO EAT
ONCE THE WOOD IS STACKED
ONCE THE NEIGHBORHOOD HERO CAN SLEEP
HIS BOAT PUT AWAY
THERE WILL BE BANDS

HOUMA, CHOCTAW
TUNICA-BILOXI, POARCH CREEK
JENNA, CHITIMACHA, COUSHATTA
WATER IS PUMPED BACK INTO THE LAKE
AWAY
TOURIST AREAS MORE OR LESS INTACT
WE ARE TOLD WHAT
"NO ONE PREDICTED"

IN AN EMERGENCY
WE SHOULD KNOW WE'RE COUSINS
REMEMBER YOUR INSTRUCTIONS PEOPLE

THERE WILL BE PARTIES
THERE WILL BE ANSWERS
IF NOT FROM THEM, FROM US
WHEN GATORS ARE COAXED BACK
HISSING LIKE KETTLES
INTO BAYOU GRASS
WHEN GRANDMA PLANS NEXT YEARS BASKET PATTERN
SOMETHING DRAMATIC ABOUT WATER, SURELY
WHEN WASHBOARDS ARE RINSED
CLEAR OF BRACKISH BOURBON-FLAVORED MUD
WHEN NEW VIOLINS ARE NEWLY STRUNG
WHEN COTTON MOUTH SOLDIERS
THOUGHT INTO BEING BY THE THUNDER BOYS
RETREAT
WE WILL SING YOU STORY
WILL WEAVE YOU SONGS
NOTES
CROSSINGS
INCANTATIONS
PERSUASIONS
PERCUSSIONS
GUIDE YOU HOME
IT IS OUR MOST IMPORTANT JOB
WITH WORDS OR WITHOUT
THERE WILL BE SONGS ABOUT THIS

CULTURALLY SENSITIVE EDUCATION

I MIGHT TAKE YOUR HISTORY BOOK
LATER THIS FALL TO A
STONE MORTAR
NEAR THE CREEK
POUND IT WITH
ACORNS
FROM A TAN OAK TO
MEAL

RUN IT WITH COLD
WATER
FROM THAT CREEK
LEACH TANNINS
LEACH INK
UNTIL THE MEAL WON'T
BURN IN MY MOUTH
UNTIL IT TASTES CLEAN

I COULD STONE BOIL THE RESULT
DAMP FROM GOOD WATER
WASHED FREE OF TOXINS
DUST IT WITH SALMON FLOUR
IT COULD BECOME SOMETHING USEFUL
COULD BE COAXED
INTO SOUP
A THING I AM FINALLY WILLING TO FEED MY CHILDREN

LESSON ON PACKING LIGHT

I DREAM OF LEARNING
CHECKERS FROM ULISI
WHO GIGGLED AS WE TEASED THE DOG
WITH A TENNIS BALL
BETWEEN MOVES
A MYSTERY TO ME THESE DAYS
WHO, IN THAT SMALL TOWN, EVER PLAYED TENNIS?
I DON'T THINK I INVENTED THE BALL THOUGH
OFF ON A TANGENT I IMAGINE IT
BOUNCING DOWN THE WILL ROGER'S TURNPIKE
TOWARDS
INDIAN HOUSING
GRAM'S DOG
OUR CHECKERS GAME
BARCALOUNGER
EXOTIC TRAPPINGS OF
MY FATHER'S FAMILY
BRIGHT ORANGE METAPHOR
CONGESTED WITH
DOG SPIT
MUD
ETTA MAE'S ELDERLY GIGGLES
THE MAGIC OF A WOMAN WITH THREE NAMES
IT FIT SO NEATLY
INTO THE DOG'S MOUTH

FIRST GOOD RAIN OF THE SEASON

WITH A SOUND THAT STARTS TO REMIND ME OF
RATTLESNAKES
THE NEIGHBOR'S AUTOMATIC SPRINKLER GOES ON
I DON'T KNOW WHAT HE'S WATERING
NOR CAN I DECODE THE TIMING
INTERVALS OF EVERY OTHER PRIME
IN SEQUENCE PERHAPS

IT'S RAINING
ON THIS ANNIVERSARY OF THE RUSSIAN REVOLUTION
RAINING
AS I PREPARE FOR A MEETING
I PULL ON WARMER BOOTS
PULL OUT A THICKER JACKET
THE SPRINKLER GOES ON AGAIN

RIVERS COME TOGETHER, GEORGIA

EVENTUALLY YOU GET DOWN TO THE HUM
SONG SLOUGHING BITS OF EVERYTHING
PUSH YOUR FINGERS THROUGH
MUD OF HUMAN STORY
MUD OF CREATION
OF PALM'S CARESS

GNAW PLUM FROM STONE
MUSCLE FROM BONE
GET TO
SACRED WATER I STAND IN NOW
IT HAS KNOWN MY FAMILY FOR
THOUSANDS OF YEARS

I WRITE ABOUT WATER OFTEN AND
WITH HER CONDITIONAL PERMISSION
SHE'LL HAND YOU BACK THE MYTH
WHAT'S LEFT OVER FROM BITS YOU WEAVE
INTO REWORKED BIOGRAPHY WITH
INK AND PULP

SHE KNOWS YOU IN ALL YOUR
UNCOMFORTABLE MAMMALNESS
WAYS IN WHICH YOU PROCESS
STRIP IT ALL AWAY
BACK TO THE HUM
SHE'LL TELL YOU ABOUT YOURSELF

DECEMBER 2005

DREAM OF INDOOR FLOODS
WAKE TO WIND
WHAT PASSES FOR STORM HERE
BRIEF UNSATISFYING FLASHES
LIMITED BOOM

RAIN WILL TATTOO
TANNIN PRINTS ONTO
CONCRETE
BY NEXT WEDNESDAY
LEAVES ARE GONE

I CAN'T LIVE
FULL EMERGENCY
I FORGET THINGS AT
FAST FORWARD
THOUGH I KEEP TRYING

ON THAT MORNING

SUNRISE JUST AFTER 7AM
FOG TO THE GROUND
NO WAY TO TELL THIS
HOUSE LIES IN THE CUP OF A CITY
FLOWER
UNFOLDING IN MY GARDEN
CREAM WITH DARK PURPLE VEINING
FINCHES
EAT PLUM BLOSSOM PETALS BUT
AVOID THIS MEAL
GIFT FROM NORTHERN MEXICO SHE
CONDUIT FOR SPEAKING WITH THE DEAD
AROUND NOON I
GO SIT
SING TO HER
DON'T WANT TO PESTER LOVED ONES WITH
QUESTIONS BUT
JUST SAY HI
SING
SPILL SAGE TEA NEAR HER ROOTS
SING

SOME OF MY COUSINS CAN

ONLY PRAY
DURING DRY YEARS
DAMS SHIFTING THE SACRED
SOMETIMES THEY SING FOR
LESS RAIN
FOR
WATER DRAINING FROM CAVES ON
MARGINS

MUD CRUMBLES WITH AND WITHOUT WATER HER
BREATH A DIFFERENT METER
LEADS AIR
LEADS WORD
WE SET OUR OWN PRAYER THERE
IN THE SEA CAVE ON THE
FIRST OF THIS NEW YEAR
COLLIDE WITH
WATER DRIVEN AIR

LEAVE DUST FROM MILES AWAY
LEAVE A TIP OF FINGERNAIL
DRIED LEAVES
CIRCLE WITH CAREFUL FEET
CARESS GROUND WITH THE
OUTSIDE CURVE
GUEST FEET
RESPECTFUL
BREATHE

DUET

STILL HAVEN'T WASHED IT AWAY
PINK DUST OF PINK SAND
STUCK WITH ME ALL THE WAY FROM
NABATEAN CISTERNS
NEAR YOUR FAMILY'S HOME
SING MORNING TO A SKY
NEARLY THE SAME COLOR
JUST AT THE HORIZON
READ YOUR WORDS UNDER THAT PINK
READ HEADLIGHTS ON THE BRIDGE
READ SIDEWALK CONCRETE
WHORL PATTERNS ECHOING
STONE COLORS IN PETRA
READ YOUR WORDS AND A
SLIGHT BREEZE BRINGS
PLUM BLOSSOM SMELL
PINK AGAIN IF
DARKER, HEAVIER
SO FAR BUT THE
SONG PRAYERS
SONG MAPS CAN
REACH JUST
FAR
ENOUGH
TUFT OF FUR
BANDED FEATHER

ANOTHER MORNING PRAYER

THERE IS THIS FEBRUARY
FROST ON THE ROOFLINES
CAR HOODS
BORED SUNLIGHT
ROSY IN THE HOUR AFTER SUNUP
PLAYING ON A WINDOW
REFLECTS AN IMAGE OF
STAR RUBIES ON THE NEXT HOUSE OVER
DON'T SPIN MY EYES
TODAY I MIGHT NEED CLARITY

CLOSE

FORGET-ME-NOT BUDS
TIGHT AS INSECT EGGS
BARELY A HINT OF BLUE RIMMED LIPS
JUST TIGHT
CLOSE
NO AMOUNT OF PRAYING
DANCING, SONG
WILL HOLD BACK RAIN NOW AND
I'M ALREADY A MARSH
IT'S THAT BLUE THAT WILL HAUNT YOU
EVEN THE RAINBOW LIT DROPS
IN THE RED LEAFED PLUM
WON'T QUITE FILL IT
EVERY COLOR BUT AND
IT'S ALREADY MARCH

SUICIDE RACCOONS

MILES UP THE COAST
RAINWATER PUSHING
MUD
TREES
OFF CLIFFS INTO THE PACIFIC
SLIDE NEAR RUSSIAN RIVER
SENDS US HOURS OUT OF THE WAY
VISIT OTHER
PARTS OF THE VALLEY
GOODBYE OF THE EMPTY BARN ON THE LEFT THEN
SUICIDE RACCOONS
SWAGGER ACROSS THE ROAD
FINALLY WE FIND THE RIGHT COPSE OF TREES
CAN'T GET THE HEAT ON FAST ENOUGH

TALECRUMBS I LEFT MYSELF FOR NAVIGATION

OFFER UP THESE STORIES LIKE
SKINNED CORN
MADE READY FOR SOUP AND
I AM HOME
THAT PLACE I WORKED SO HARD TO CREATE
SOMEWHERE BETWEEN THOSE RIVERS
PAPA'S SCAB KNUCKLED HANDS
HERO'S HANDS
POLISH GRANDMA'S EVERYTHING STEW
GRAINS OF RICE CURLING LIKE SOMETHING I WOULD
LATER CALL
FLEUR-DE-LIS
ALMOST GUILTY JOY OF BOOKS
CUP OF TEA, BLANKET AND A BOOK
SITTING NEAR THE HEATER
SUCH DELICATE CONSTRUCTIONS
COMPLEX AND FRAGILE
JUST ABOUT
NEARLY A HOME
THINGS THAT WERE SAVED
BACON DRIPPING
BREAD BAG TIES
COFFEE JARS WITH COMMEMORATIVE LETTERING
LATER USED TO STORE DRIED APPLES THAT WOULD
TASTE OF COFFEE
SUMMER HEAT OF OKLAHOMA
SOMETHING I NEED FROM LOVERS THESE DAYS
WET HEAT
WITH SOMETIME DIPS INTO COLDER WATER
WE FIND WAYS HOME
DON'T WE JUST

KID GAME

I PLAYED HIDE AND SEEK
BECAUSE I WANTED SOMEONE TO FIND ME
LAYING UNDER THE STAIRS
OF THE HOUSE TWO DOORS UP
AS A HIDING SPOT IT WAS
MORE A SLIGHT OF HAND
TRICK OF THE ANGLE
THAN ANY REAL
NOOK OF CONCEALMENT
I'D EVEN LAUGH SOMETIMES
WHEN THE OTHER KIDS WOULD RUN OVER ME
BUT THEY NEVER LOOKED PROPERLY
JUST USING THEM TO GET TO OTHER
BETTER KNOWN SPOTS AND
ALTHOUGH I WANTED IT MORE THAN ANYONE
I WAS NEVER FOUND

ATSINA

IT'S NOT THE SOUTH COAST
MOANING GREEN
VOICE OF THE CLIFFSIDE
SHATTERED LIKE A MIRROR
CHORUS OF THOUSANDS
ONE NOTE
OCTAVE LOWER HUM OF PINES
CHIPPED WIND
IT'S NOT THAT OTHER GREEN
UNDERGROUND
TRACED UP WITH THE
HORSETAIL
OR CRACK OF DRY FERNS
AFTER THE STORM
NOT LOW FOG
NOT STUMPS BLAZING MOSS
NOT ABALONE SCRAPS
NOT WARM TREES HUNG WITH LICHEN
FINALLY IT IS THE WOODSMOKE
SMELLING OF GOOD BRUSH INK IN
LATE AFTERNOON

MINOR 9TH AT THE JAZZ CONCERT

AS IF LONGING WERE ONLY FOR WOMEN OR IT
CAME IN FLAVORS THAT
REQUIRE SOME GENETIC ABILITY TO TASTE IT'S A
CASE OF IRRATIONAL RATIOS
DOWNBEATS HOLD IT ALL TOGETHER
QUIRKS OF LANGUAGE WE
MAY HAVE FORGOTTEN LIKE
ABSTRACT GESTURES ON THE DINNER TABLE THE
SIDE DISH THAT YOU LEAVE OUT WHEN YOU
CAREFULLY COPY THE CASSEROLE SHE
ALWAYS SERVED LIMA BEANS IN THE
SKY-BLUE BOWL WE USED TO HULL STRAWBERRIES INTO
IT I
FOUND MYSELF TYING A BERRY COLORED SCARF OVER
THE
BLUE SHIRT I'D CHOSEN FOR THE SHOW THIS
BEAT WILL MAKE ITSELF HEARD THINGS YOU
DIDN'T KNOW YOU WERE LEARNING AS IF
LONGING WERE JUST FOR WOMEN AS IF THE THING
COULD ONLY BE PRESENTED PROPERLY AS A
SIDE DISH AND ONLY
IN A BLUE BOWL WITH A CRACKLED GLAZE

LOVE SONG

THIS IS WOMEN'S WORK TOO THIS
WASHING OF THE DEAD IT
NEVER ENDS
PRAYER AND WATER
FOAM AND WATER THEN A
CLICHÉD NOTE A SMEAR OF DUST IT'S
HOMEOPATHY SHE'S
GONE IN EVERY RESPECT ALMOST A
CURE FOR THE PERSON SHE ONCE WAS AND
LIKE OTHER CURES WE NEVER WANTED TO TAKE IT
COULD BE BITTER BUT THERE
SHE IS IN THE
HANDS OF THE WOMAN WHO WASHES THE DEAD THIS
TRUE BELIEVER A
LAST THING THAT I CAN'T DO

MYTH OF THE IMMIGRANT

THERE ARE THESE STRAIGHT LINES ON PAPER THEY
HAVE A KIND OF MAGIC
BESTOW AUTHORITY THAT
SEEMS TO OVERCOME THAT OF
RIVERS
HISTORY BEFORE THE SOLDIERS A
PALM PRINT
BLOOD TYPE

NOT ANONYMOUS
MYTH OF THE IMMIGRANT AN EXCUSE TO
FAIL IN SACRED RESPONSIBILITIES A
RISK THEY SEEM WILLING TO TAKE WHEN IT
FLOODS SOMEONE ELSE'S NEIGHBORHOOD
BURNS SOMEONE ELSE'S HOUSE
EXPOSES AUSTRALIA TO A GREATER RISK OF
SKIN CANCER

WORDS DON'T GET SHOPWORN
JUST THE IDEAS THEY REPRESENT
WE GET TIRED
BECAUSE THEY KEEP TELLING A TIRESOME STORY
TIRED OF THE PLAUSIBLE LIES THAT
QUICKLY BECOME IMPLAUSIBLE AS
JUST OVER THE BORDER
INDIAN WOMEN ARE STILL BEING MURDERED DAILY

TOO MANY AFTERNOONS OF RAIN AND
GLOBAL WARMING ISN'T REAL OR
SO THEY SAY BUT THIS
MORNING AN EAST WIND TOLD ME OTHERWISE THE
JAY AND I HUMMING THE SUN UP TOGETHER
CALL UP THE RIVERS, PUT ON YOUR SINGING CLOTHES
CHANT THE NAMES OF EACH COUSIN WE HAVE
UNSTITCH THESE BOUNDARIES

I ALWAYS CATCH THE OLD WORLD DISEASES

I'M POST-COLUMBIAN
INHERIT THE CRACKLE AND
RESIDUE OF THE MUD HANDED INVADERS AND
MEASLES THAT I NEVER DEVELOP A RESISTANCE TO
OH
I'VE HAD THOSE SHOTS BUT STILL CATCH THE DISEASE
EACH TIME IT ENTERS ME IT
COULD HAVE BEEN MY BLOND GRANDFATHER'S FAULT
SALT MINER THAT HE WAS HE
HELD A UNION POST DURING THE
GENERAL STRIKE IT COULD BE A
SCRAP OF HIS CODE THAT
OPENS THOSE DOORS A
CONFLATION OF ALWAYS AND NEVER I
WAS HIS PRINCESS WITH MY GLOW-IN-THE-DARK
BABY SKIN MY
SOGGY HANDS EVEN THEN
BLUE-COLLAR SQUARE
SNAPPING THE CLIP EARRINGS ONTO HIS
WHITE FURRED EARS
BOORISH A
STUDENT SAID OF ME
COMPLAINED OF STORIES FROM MY
UNLIKELY LIFE BUT I AM UNLIKELY
POST-COLUMBIAN NDN
HILL-BILLY POLISH
UNION AGITATOR AND CAREER MILITARY DNA AN
INHERITANCE FROM MY GRANDFATHERS
BORN TO TAKE THE BULLET
TAKE THE GERM
TAKE THE WEIGHT ON MY
WORKING CLASS SHOULDERS MY
NATIVE FEET

MINING TOWN

THEY WERE THE HEARTH ENDS THE
ONES WHO GREW UP IN THAT HOUSE
LEAD MINERS BY DAY UNTIL 4PM
BRANCH HOBOS
WOULD DROP A HOOKED LINE INTO EVERY BIT OF
WATER IN THE COUNTY
COME HOME TO SHARED BEDS AND FRIED CATFISH THE
OTHER PRODUCT OF THEIR LABORS
WOULD PUT COAL INTO THE POTBELLY
HEAT IT AS RED HOT AS THE
MELTING FURNACE AT WORK
UNTIL THE FIRE LIFTED THEM
SMALL ROUNDED BITS OF LEAD THEMSELVES AND
FLUNG THEM FROM THE FLAMES

MUD AND WORDS

TRYING TO FIND THE WORD THAT
CAN HOLD OFF THE WATER
HOLD UP A TOWN
JUST ONE MORE WORD
ANOTHER WAY TO ASK THAT PEOPLE
PAY ATTENTION THERE IS
WORK TO BE DONE HERE AND
THERE
PEOPLE FLOODED
MONEY FOR THE LEVEE USED FOR
BULLETS USED TO WAGE COMMERCE
OFF SOMEWHERE IN THAT DIRECTION
NOT WHERE THAT MONEY BELONGED AND THE
MAPS ARE VAGUE BUT FAR TOO DETAILED
LEVEES FALLING FROM THE WEIGHT OF THE WATER WE'LL
SING THOSE PEOPLE MORNING SONGS AND SEND THEM
ANOTHER BLESSING
LOCUSTS IN THE DAY AND
CRICKETS AT NIGHT THEN A
SMALL TOWN IN OKLAHOMA IS
SINKING INTO THE MINES THAT WERE
DUG FOR ANOTHER WAR EFFORT
LEAD FOR BULLETS THAT
WOUND UP IN TREES ON ISLANDS OFF THAT WAY
TREES ON HILLSIDES OFF THE OTHER WAY
WOUND UP IN ENEMY SOLDIERS
NOT WHERE THAT LEAD BELONGED AND NOW
EVERYTHING FALLING FROM THE WEIGHT OF THE
LIVING
WE CAN TRY TO HOLD WATER WITH A SIEVE OF WORDS
SINK WORDS OF STRENGTH INTO THE DIRT
JUST INSIDE THE KANSAS BORDER
PAY ATTENTION PEOPLE
JUST ONE MORE VERB HERE
NOUN UNDER THE TREE ROOTS
MUD AND A HANDFUL OF CONJUNCTIONS
SLAPPED ONTO THE NEW LEVEE
PAY ATTENTION
YOU WILL KNOW THE POETS BY THE
DIRT UNDER OUR NAILS

OPENING GLOW

HARD TO KNOW WHAT HEAT
WILL SPRING YOU
OPEN IF YOU ARE A PINECONE
HERE IN THE CITY
COULD BE SOME RANDOM
ATMOSPHERIC EVENT
PRYING WOODEN SCALES WIDE THE
KIND OF DAY THAT SENDS PEOPLE
RUNNING FOR THE SHADE OF TALL BUILDINGS
CRACKLES THE PINES ON CAMPUS
WRACKING THE NERVES OF
PASSERS UNDERNEATH OR IT
COULD BE MY GAS STOVE
SET LOW TO A FANTASY OF PINONS
SO THAT WE CAN BOTH TASTE HOME

DREAM SKY

THINGS JUST FLY EVERYWHERE
DON'T THEY?
MOMS TAKE OFF FROM THE BEACH
SMALL AIRCRAFT IN A SPACE WHERE
YOU CAN CONTROL COLORS
YELLOW TO BLUE WITH YOUR PITCH AND
ROLL
MEANWHILE LARGE MAMMALS FLOAT BY
SPOTTED FUR COVERING
MUSCLES THAT CONTROL
IMPULSES I DON'T KNOW
HOW COULD FLUKES FEEL?
SWIM WITHOUT DELIBERATION
THROUGH AIR
SOMETIMES A
THING WITH HORNS
I'M TOO SLEEPY THESE DAYS
TO BE TRICKY
TORE THE MASK OFF OF ONE MONSTER SHE WAS
CHASING ME
I ASKED HER TO DINNER
COULDN'T SPEND ENERGY ON PURSUIT
I HAD TO GRADE TESTS IN THE MORNING
MEANWHILE THE BOOKS REPRODUCE IN THE

BEDROOM
LIVING ROOM
EVERYTHING SINGS GREEN IF I DON'T PAY ATTENTION

EFFECTS OF COLONIALISM
A PRAYER OF HEALING FOR EVERYONE... TO BE SUNG WITH MARY JEAN

THIS HILL IS STILL LEARNING ENGLISH.
IF YOU TRY TO PRAY WITH IT HERE
GO SLOW
OR SHE MIGHT NOT UNDERSTAND YOU.

MY ANCESTOR MADE POEMS
THERE IS ONE ABOUT BLUE AND WHITE.
SKIN THAT TOLD A STORY OF CHALK CLIFFS
VEINS MAPPING RIVERS SHE DIDN'T KNOW.
I THINK SHE SWIPED HIM OFF OF A BOAT.
I NOT SURE SHE EVER
GAVE HIM BACK.

THERE IS AN ILLEGAL SETTLEMENT OF
CELLS IN THAT WOMAN'S SKIN.
DESPITE POLITICAL PRESSURE THE CELLS
WILL NOT DISMANTLE THEIR VILLAGE.
THERE ARE RUMBLINGS
TALK OF EXTREME ACTION.
WE MIGHT BOMBARD THEM.
WE WILL CERTAINLY WRITE NASTY THINGS ABOUT THEM.
THIS MATERIAL MAY WELL BE SUPPRESSED BY
THE PARTISAN PRESS.

GRAM SAID:
'EVERYTHING YOU NEED TO HEAL YOU
IS WITHIN 10 FEET OF WHERE YOU STAND.'
I WONDER IF IT'S STILL TRUE.
EVERYTHING GETS MOVED AROUND SO MUCH
THESE DAYS.
HAVE TO PUT TOGETHER THE PUZZLE OF LOCATION.
FIND OUR OWN ROSELINE.
STAND STILL
WE CAN LOOK TOGETHER.

TALKING STORY

SPEAKS LIKE PICKING
RIPE APPLES
TIME TO ADMIRE
ROSESHINE ON THE CHEEK OF ONE
THE ANGLE OF AN
ACCOMPANYING LEAF
SUN WARM
THICK WITH MORNING STEAM
ORIGINAL APPLES
INNOCENT OF HUMAN
TINKERING
STRIKES ME THAT
THIS STORY
WON'T END
JUST CIRCLE THROUGH
APPLE TREES
AROUND MIDDAY THERE IS A
BREAK
BY EVENING WE ARE
POKING THROUGH
THE BOWL
AGAIN
CHOOSING JUST ONE
A TOUCH CHALKY
TO SET ON THE BEDSIDE
TABLE TO
WAIT FOR A
MORNING
PRE-KISS
BITE

ZERO

I'M A PRETTY GOOD SHOT
ENJOY SEEING THE BOTTLES EXPLODE
IT'S A GRIM SLIGHT OF HAND
BUT SATISFYING.
DON'T IMAGINE FOR A MOMENT
THAT I'M A PACIFIST.
I CAN THINK OF THINGS THAT WOULD MAKE ME KILL A
PERSON.
I KNOW OF PEOPLE WHO WOULD DO THEM.
MY REQUIREMENTS FOR THAT HAVEN'T BEEN MET IN MY
SEEING
SO I'LL STICK TO THE BOTTLES.

THE LOGIC OF A BODY CAN BE TYRANNY.
CELLS CREATED, LINKED IN
VIBRATION
MUSIC
INHERENT SENSE OF BEAUTY.
OVERALL AN EQUATION WHOSE SUM IS
ZERO.
WE ARE ALWAYS FINDING THAT THINGS ARE MORE
COMPLICATED
THAN WE ORIGINALLY THOUGHT.
IF YOU AREN'T DELIGHTED YOU AREN'T PAYING
ATTENTION.

THE BOY IN ME LIKES THE MEASUREMENTS
THE BIG NOISES
BITS OF GLASS FLYING IN ALL DIRECTIONS.
I ENJOY PERCUSSIVE ANSWERS
A DRUM ROLL OF SAXON CONSONANTS
THE CHEMISTRY OF MY OWN MUSCLES.
HOW BIG, HOW FAR, HOW FAST?
I LIKE THE MATH OF CONFLICT.
SWEAT IS GOOD
A CHEMISTRY LINKING EVERYTHING.

FIREWORKS
SHADOW NEURONS FIRING.
WHERE DOES THE CHEMICAL
EASE INTO THE ELECTRICAL?
WHAT STRANGE CORTICAL CONNECTION
BETWEEN
SHARDS OF GLASS
AND MY PALM
BREATHING THROUGH
THE RECOIL?

FEAR OF HEIGHTS

TRIP OVER IN SLEEP
FALL AWAKE
NO LIGHT ON THE HORIZON
CAN'T GET ENOUGH WEIGHT
TO STAY ON THE GROUND
HEAD FOR THE AIRSHED
WHERE THE WINDS CHANGE DIRECTION
BUOYANCY REVERSES
SEA AND BAY AIR
CRASH
WITH
COASTAL MOUNTAIN AIR
AND EARTH IS REACHABLE

AGAIN THE NEXT DAY
FEEL FEET
LIFTING
OFF THE FLOOR
30 RAPT CHILDREN
WATCH THE
STRUGGLE FOR BALLAST
BREATHE GROUNDING AIR
CULTURE OF THE SCHOOL
HOLDS ME DOWN
STUDENTS
DOUBT WHAT THEY SEE
A LONG WALK HOME

STORM WIND
FINALLY IN OFF THE
BAY
THAT EVENING
WINDOW THOUGHTFUL
PRECAUTIONS ARE SENSIBLE
ACCIDENTAL FLIGHT
COULD
LEAD ANYWHERE
NO PILL FOR THIS
FORGET TO BE HEAVY
FALL AWAKE
PEEL AWAY

FLOOD SINGING

STANDING HERE SURROUNDED BY WET WOOD
DEAD REFRIGERATORS WE
MUST FINALLY ADMIT
THERE IS NO MYSTERY HERE IT'S A
HABIT OF SPEECH
CLICHÉ AS IF
INDIFFERENCE WAS THE WEATHER I
HAVE A DOWSER'S HEADACHE BUT
DON'T HAVE A SOUP POT BIG ENOUGH TO
RIDE OVER NOW NOT FLOODED STREETS A
WILD WOMAN IN A CHICKEN FOOT HUT
MAKING AN OLD MAGIC
PASSING OUT A MEAL
BOWL OF SOMETHING MY OTHER GRAN
WOULD HAVE CALLED
OGAMA
THICK WITH SQUASH WITH
GROUND SPICEBUSH
BROOMS AND BRICK DUST MY
HOPE FOR YOUR PATH FROM THIS
MOMENT
CHANT NAILS, NEW ROOFS AND SNUGNESS TO
STREAKS OF PINK AND BLUE IN THE
EASTERN SKY I
SING OF YOUR NEW HOUSES THEY ARE
COMING I HEAR THEM
RESTITCH QUILTS OF NEIGHBORHOOD FROM
CLOTHES WE FOUND FLOATING IN THE LAKE
WE HAVE SUCH FOCUS THE NEEDLES MAGNETIZE WE
USE THEM TO
FIND EACH OTHER

CLOUDS RUNNING IN

SULLEN SLOW THESE
BATTLES ALONG THE ARTERIES IN THE
VEINS ARE
CALCULATED DROP BY DROP IT'S HOW THAT
RULE ALWAYS WORKED THEY HOPE THEY CAN
SLICE IT FINER THAN THEIR SCIENCE CAN
CALCULATE BECAUSE THEY DON'T REALLY
WANT TO KNOW THE ANSWERS

SOON THEY'LL DROP YET
ANOTHER BOMB ON
NEWE SOGOBIA
STARVE MORE IMPOUNDED
HORSES TO DEATH OUR
SACRED FOOD ISN'T THE SAME WE ARE
MADE OF DIFFERENT STUFF BUT FOR YOU
I WILL SING THOSE SELU SONGS THAT I CAN REMEMBER

IT COULD BE TOO MUCH FIRE UNDERGROUND OR
TOO MUCH WATER BUT
EITHER WAY WE NEED AN EAR TO IT
DELIBERATE IGNORANCE IS COMPLICITY
I BELIEVE IN FORGIVENESS
ONLY IN THE MOMENT BEFORE THE
NEXT ATTACK
SOMETIMES EVEN THEN THERE ISN'T TIME

PEOPLE DROWN IN THE DESERT IT ISN'T A
METAPHOR FOR SOCIAL CHANGE
A MATTER OF WATER DOING WATER THINGS
TRY NOT TO WALK IN THE
DRY WASH IT DOESN'T
STAY DRY IT'S NOT
RAINING YET BUT
CAN YOU HEAR THE CLOUDS RUNNING IN?

MAKING NOISES

LOUD WEATHER FOR A WEEK
SOMETIMES WE JUST GET TOSSED
RAIN, WIND-MUSCLE
EVERYTHING SHAKES

OUT ON THE MOUNTAIN THEY'RE CLIMBING BLIND
WITH SO MANY COMPRESSIVE CURRENT EVENTS
SO MUCH TO FORTIFY AGAINST
I'M SUDDENLY DRAWN ALONG BY
REAL BRAVERY
DRAWN UP
HEAD ACHING
FROM THE ALTITUDE
THIS IS LOUD TOO
THIS BEING FLUNG IN WITH A HOPEFUL THOUGHT
I FOLLOW THE SLOPE FROM A DISTANCE
WRACKED WITH SYMPATHY JOY

IT'S LOUD
LARGE WITH SLOW EARTH CONTRACTIONS
THE MAKING AND UNMAKING OF LAND
TWISTING GROAN OF ANOTHER SPASM

I WANT TO TRUST IN THE IMPULSE
TEAR DOWN THE CRENELLATIONS
BUT THEY'VE REBUILT THEM
AND MORE THAN ONCE
A REFLEX, HUMANITY MAYBE
PILES OF ROCK
SHARPENED SUGAR POINTS
FLAKED PATIENTLY
TO A FLINT DEADLINESS
VANISH IN THE BLOOD
DENIABLE
COMPLICATED, TRANSLUCENT AND CORROSIVE

BUT NO, IN THIS MOMENT OF
EXPANDING
WITHOUT CONTAINMENT WE PICK A NOTE
AND GET REALLY LOUD

CITY SHOES -DANCING FOG

IN SOME SPECIES OF LIGHT
BLACK
IF YOU DON'T LISTEN
OR CAN'T HEAR THE
BLUE HUM
WE PULL ON OUR CITY SHOES, CARS SOLES PAINTED LIKE
TIRE TREAD

FOG BLOWS IN HARD
PRETENDS IT'S RAIN
SO THE TREES DRIP
SOME NIGHTS
LOUDER THAN THE CITY SOUNDS
WE ARE ALL ABOUT WATER ON THIS PENINSULA

TRIPLE POINT OF HUMAN OCCUPATION, THIS
CITY
COUNTRY
SUBURB
A NEIGHBOR LEADS A GOAT
ON A LEASH

TONIGHT WE'RE EATING FLOWERS
PULLING ON CITY SHOES
DUST EACH OTHER WITH EUCALYPTUS POLLEN, ANOTHER
NATURALIZED NEWCOMER
WE DANCE FOG
SING FOG
AN OFFERING TO THE SPIRIT OF THE PLACE

THE WAY WE HONOR HEROIC PONIES IN THE CITY

THE ANNIVERSARY OF THE GREAT LOCUST SWARM
I'M BEADING YOUR TRUCK
ONTO THE HEEL OF MY DANCE SHOES
SPENT MONTHS LOOKING FOR THE RED
DRIVEN THE CENTRAL VALLEY RED
PARKED IN THE SUN AT THE MILLS POW WOW RED
ACCIDENTALLY LEFT UNLOCKED IN DOWNTOWN
OAKLAND AND
NOT RIFLED RED
RED OF SHARED PLUMS AND COOKIES
RED OF MAGIC FURNITURE MOVING
RED
IN THE CURVE OF HELPING OTHER PEOPLE
OF MOVING CAMP
OF REPEATED REPAIR
SUPERMAN RED

ARTIFICIAL STONE

THAT SNAKE IS BACK THE
ONE WHOSE SCALES ARE
STOLEN FROM LACEBARK PINE CONES
WHOSE EYES ARE PATCHY
BROWN AND GREY
WON'T MATTER HOW HARD I WORK TODAY HE
TENDS TO SWALLOW THE GOOD BITS
SAVES THEM TILL LATER WHEN I
NEVER SEEM TO REMEMBER WHERE I WAS GOING OR
MAYBE HE STRIPS THEM OF ALL LANDMARKS
PEELS THE CRACKS OUT OF THE SIDEWALK AND
BY BEING HERE
BY TAKING HIS RATTLE STARS
FROM THE CATALOG OF NIGHT STORY
DISTORTS MY MAP AND I
CAN'T EVEN FIND MY WAY HOME

Kim Shuck has held many jobs from dispensing health food sweets and coffee to being an assistant teacher in a modern dance studio to gluing rhinestones onto plastic mesh. Her first professional poetry publication was in the En'Owken Journal and her most recent was in Avatar Review. Kim's initial full solo book, Smuggling Cherokee, won the Diane Decorah award from the Native Writer's Circle of the Americas in 2005. She has also won a mentor of the year award from Wordcraft Circle of Native Writers and Storytellers, a Mary Tall Mountain award and various other awards and publications in journals, periodicals and anthologies. Kim volunteers with second graders every week disguising math as art and art as math, she has been part of the San Francisco poetry scene for the last twenty mumble years and her beadwork can be seen every weekend during pow wow season from North Carolina to Fresno. She edits the infrequent Rabbit and Rose online literary journal, lives in San Francisco with one of her two sons, a housecoat, a small feline she thought was a housecoat when she adopted it and a grumpy and mouthy parrot named Bond.

DRAWINGS BY MARCER CAMPBELL

MARCER CAMPBELL PAINTS AND DRAWS IN A WAY THAT MAKES ME WANT TO WRITE. WE'VE BEEN DOING COLLABORATIONS AS A SORT OF CALL AND RESPONSE FOR AWHILE NOW. THIS COLLECTION IS MORE MARCER RESPONDING TO MY WRITING BUT WE STARTED OUT DOING EXACTLY THE OPPOSITE, WITH ME RESPONDING IN POEM TO HIS PAINTINGS. MARCER IS FROM CUMBRIA IN THE FAR NORTH OF ENGLAND AND NOW LIVES ON THE OTHER SIDE OF THE BORDER IN SCOTLAND. HIS UNDERSTANDING OF THE ENVIRONMENTS HE PAINTS HAS BEEN ABSORBED THROUGH EVERY PORE AND STUDIED WITH AN INCREASINGLY TRAINED EYE OVER THE COURSE OF HIS LIFETIME. THE WORDS THAT I WOULD PICK TO DESCRIBE HIS WORK WOULD ONLY MAKE HIM BLUSH, BUT I CONSIDER IT AN OVERWHELMING PRIVILEGE TO SHARE SPACE IN THIS BOOK WITH HIM. GO SEE OUR OTHER COLLABORATIONS AND MORE OF HIS PAINTINGS AND DRAWINGS AT HTTP://MARCERCAMPBELL.CO.UK